The Nature Kid's Guide to
DRAGONFLIES

DAVID ANDERSON

LP Media Inc. Publishing
Text copyright © 2026 by LP Media Inc.
All rights reserved.

For information address LP Media Inc. Publishing,
30012 Variolite St NW, Princeton MN 55371
www.lpmedia.org

Publication Data

Dragonflies
The Nature Kid's Guide to Dragonflies — First edition.

Summary: "Learn all about Dragonflies, the Nature Kid Way"
— Provided by publisher.

ISBN: 979-8-89818-196-3

[1. Dragonflies – Non-Fiction] I. Title.

Title: The Nature Kid's Guide to Dragonflies

CONTENTS

MEET THE DRAGONFLY

Ancient dragonflies had wings stretching over two feet wide— bigger than a hawk's!

Zip! A dragonfly zooms past your face in a blur of wings.

That blur is a dragonfly — and it is one of the most incredible hunters on the planet. These tiny fliers have been darting through the sky for over 300 million years!

Dragonflies live near water on every continent except Antarctica. They come in almost every color imaginable — red, blue, green, gold, and purple. Some are smaller than your thumbnail. Others stretch wider than your hand.

But do not let their size fool you. Dragonflies are the most accurate hunters on the planet — and this book is going to show you exactly how!

WING WIZARDS

A dragonfly has about 30,000 tiny lenses in each eye—you only have one lens per eye!

Whirr! Four shiny wings lift a dragonfly into the sky.

Dragonflies have four wings, not two. Each wing moves on its own. This lets them fly up, down, backward, and even hover in place like tiny helicopters.

Huge eyes cover most of a dragonfly's head. These eyes can see in almost every direction at once, helping them spot tiny bugs from far away. Nothing sneaks up on a dragonfly.

During flight, a dragonfly tucks its legs in close. Its long, thin body twists and turns with ease. Every part of this insect is built to hunt.

PRECISION PREDATORS

Snap! A dragonfly snatches a bug just above a pond's surface.

Dragonflies almost never miss a meal. When they chase a bug, they catch it. Very few animals on Earth can match that skill.

But a dragonfly does not just chase from behind. It flies to where the bug will be next. Its brain works out the perfect path in a flash— faster than you can blink.

Then the dragonfly swoops in close. Its six spiny legs snap together like a basket to scoop up **prey**. The bug never sees it coming.

DOUBLE LIVES

A dragonfly nymph may shed its skin up to 15 times as it grows bigger and bigger!

Crack! A dragonfly nymph crawls along the sandy lake bed.

A dragonfly lives two very different lives. First, it is a **nymph**. Nymphs hatch from eggs laid in water and breathe through **gills**, just like fish.

Underwater, a nymph becomes a fierce hunter. It eats tiny bugs, worms, and even small fish. Some nymphs spend years in the water before they are ready to change.

One day, the nymph crawls out onto a plant stem. Its skin splits open, and crumpled wings slowly unfold. Now it is an adult dragonfly, ready to take to the sky.

DARNER DRIFTERS

Whoosh! A green darner races across a sunny meadow.

The Common Green Darner is found all across North America. It has a bright green chest and a sky-blue belly. Look for it near ponds and marshes on warm days.

Green darners **migrate**, just like birds do. In fall, big groups fly south to stay warm. Come spring, they head back north again. Scientists are still learning how they find their way.

These darners are strong, speedy fliers. They can reach 35 miles per hour while chasing small bugs. A green darner can fly for hours without stopping to rest.

WANDERING GLIDER

Wandering Gliders cross the Indian Ocean—a trip of over 3,700 miles with no place to land!

DID YOU KNOW?

Swoosh! A wandering glider rides the wind across the ocean.

The Wandering Glider is the greatest insect traveler on Earth. It migrates, following monsoon rains all the way across oceans and continents to find temporary pools of water to lay its eggs.

These gliders ride the wind for incredible trips. They soar over oceans, deserts, and mountains. Some journeys stretch thousands of miles, taking several generations to complete.

The secret to their success is speed. Their nymphs hatch and grow up in just six weeks — fast enough to develop before a rain puddle dries up and disappears.

FLAME FLIERS

Flash! A bright red dragonfly glows like fire by the stream.

The Flame Skimmer is easy to spot. Males have bright red or orange bodies that glow in the sun. They look like little flames dancing over the water.

These dragonflies love warm places. You can find them in the western United States, from California to Texas. They prefer sunny ponds and slow, shallow streams.

Male Flame Skimmers guard a patch of water fiercely. They chase away any other males who come too close. Females visit these guarded spots to lay their eggs in safety.

PENNANT PATROL

The Halloween Pennant can fly in wind and rain that grounds other dragonflies!

Flutter! An orange and brown dragonfly waves in the breeze.

The Halloween Pennant has orange and brown wings with bold stripes. Its colors look like a tiny flag waving in the wind. That is how it got the name pennant.

This dragonfly likes to perch on tall plants near water. It sits at the very tip and sways in the breeze. Look for it near ponds in the eastern United States.

Halloween Pennants are not shy at all. They may land right on your finger or hat. These bold little bugs do not scare easily, even when people get close.

SPOTTED SKIMMERS

Buzz! A spotted dragonfly zips from one sunny rock to another.

The Twelve-spotted Skimmer has exactly 12 dark spots on its wings—three on each wing. Males also have white patches between the spots. This bold pattern makes it easy to identify.

Look for this skimmer near calm ponds and lakes. It perches on sticks poking out of the water, watching for prey. When a bug flies past, the skimmer darts out for a quick snack.

Males guard the same patch of water all day long. They chase away any other males that dare to fly in. These skimmers do not like to share their **territory**.

DASHER DAZZLE

A male Blue Dasher may gobble up hundreds of mosquitoes in a single day!

Zing! A blue dasher sits on its perch and watches for its next meal.

The Blue Dasher is a small, common dragonfly found across North America. Males have bright blue bodies and striking green eyes. Females are tan with dark stripes down their backs.

Blue Dashers hunt by sitting and waiting. They pick a sunny perch and watch for bugs to fly past. The moment one does, the dasher zooms after it in a blur.

You can find these dragonflies near almost any pond. They show up early each spring and stay until fall. Blue Dashers are often the first dragonflies people learn to recognize.

BUTTERFLY FLUTTERER

The Butterfly Flutterer only lives in very clean water — scientists say spotting one means the wetland is healthy!

Flutter! A dragonfly with glowing blue wings lands near a marsh.

The Butterfly Flutterer lives in East Asia — in Japan, China, Taiwan, and Korea. Its wings are deep blue and iridescent, shifting color as the light hits them at different angles. No other dragonfly looks quite like it.

This dragonfly does not dart and zoom like most of its cousins. It flaps its wide wings slowly and floats through the air, looking so much like a butterfly that people often mistake it for one.

Despite its gentle flight, it is still a fierce hunter. Mosquitoes are its favorite target. It patrols ponds, marshes, and rice paddies from June to September, catching meals on the wing.

PETALTAIL GIANTS

Zoom! A huge dragonfly lands on a giant leaf. It's huge!

The Giant Petaltail is one of the biggest dragonflies alive today. It can stretch more than four inches long—about the size of your hand. Its thick body is brown with bright yellow spots.

Petaltails belong to a very ancient group. Their ancestors flew when dinosaurs walked the Earth. In many ways, these dragonflies are living fossils.

These giants live near small, boggy streams in shady forests. They hunt from low perches, waiting in the shadows. When a beetle or moth passes by, the petaltail strikes with lightning speed.

EMERALD ENIGMAS

Some emerald dragonflies fly in perfect figure-eight patterns while hunting!

Zoom! A green dragonfly glints like a gem over the pond.

Emerald dragonflies have shiny green eyes and metallic bodies. They glow like tiny jewels when sunlight hits them. Many people think they are the prettiest dragonflies of all.

These dragonflies are tricky to spot. They often fly at dawn and dusk when light is dim. Some even hunt on cloudy days when other dragonflies rest.

Emeralds live near bogs, ponds, and slow-moving rivers. They patrol the same path over and over, back and forth. Watching one is like seeing a tiny green helicopter on patrol.

MOSAIC MASTERS

Mosaic Darners sometimes hunt at night, drawn to bright porch lights!

Whizz! A colorful darner weaves through the trees at top speed.

The Mosaic Darner gets its name from its colorful body. Blue and green spots cover its dark back in a beautiful pattern. The design looks like tiny tiles arranged in a mosaic.

This darner is one of the last dragonflies flying each year. It keeps hunting late into fall, even on chilly days. You can spot it when most other dragonflies have disappeared.

Mosaic Darners hunt along trails and forest edges. They fly back and forth, scanning for bugs. Stand very still, and one might zoom right past your head.

SADDLEBAG SOARING

Black Saddlebags sometimes travel in swarms of thousands— like a dragonfly parade!

Swish! A dark dragonfly glides low over a field of tall grass.

The Black Saddlebags has dark patches on its back wings. These patches look like little saddlebags hanging on a horse. That is exactly how this dragonfly got its unusual name.

Black Saddlebags are masters at gliding. They hold their wings out wide and coast on the breeze for long stretches. You can spot them in groups near open fields and meadows.

These dragonflies travel long distances each year. When weather turns cold, they fly south in huge groups. Big swarms of them fill the autumn sky.

PINK PATROL

Male Roseate Skimmers are not born pink—they slowly turn rosy as they grow up!

Hum! A pink dragonfly floats above a sunny lily pad.

The Roseate Skimmer is one of the only pink dragonflies in the world. Males have a rosy pink body that really stands out. Females are more golden brown with hints of yellow.

This skimmer lives in warm parts of North and South America. It loves sunny ponds, lakes, and marshes with plenty of plants. Watch for it perching on sticks above the water.

Males fly over the water to show off their bright color. That pink body warns other males to stay away from their territory. It also helps attract females looking for a mate.

HEALTHY HABITATS

Splash! A dragonfly nymph drops into a clean, clear pond.

Dragonflies need clean water to survive. Their nymphs grow up in ponds, streams, and wetlands. When water gets polluted, nymphs cannot breathe or find food.

Seeing lots of dragonflies means the water is healthy. Scientists call them indicator species—they are like tiny signs that nature is doing well. Fewer dragonflies can be an early warning that something is wrong.

You can help by keeping water clean. Never toss trash near ponds or streams. Planting native flowers and bushes near water gives dragonflies places to rest and hunt.

DRAGONFLY DISCOVERY
FUN FACT!
There are over 5,000 kinds of dragonflies—and scientists discover new ones every year!
38

Zap! A dragonfly speeds by and makes you want to follow it.

You can watch dragonflies almost anywhere there is water. Ponds, lakes, and streams are great places to start. Warm, sunny days bring out the most dragonflies.

Bring a notebook and draw what you see. Notice the colors, wing patterns, and body size. These clues help you figure out what kind you found. Soon you will recognize your favorites.

Every dragonfly you spot is part of nature's story. They help keep ponds and rivers healthy by eating mosquitoes and other pests. Head outside and see how many kinds you can find!

GLOSSARY

nymph

A young dragonfly that lives in water before it grows wings

migrate

To travel a long way to find food or warmth

prey

An animal that is hunted and eaten by another animal

gills

Body parts that let an animal breathe underwater

territory

An area that an animal defends and keeps other animals out of